Magma
Intrusions

Magma Intrusions

Poems by

Meg Weston

© 2023 Meg Weston. All rights reserved.
This material may not be reproduced in any form, published,
reprinted, recorded, performed, broadcast,
rewritten or redistributed without
the explicit permission of Meg Weston.
All such actions are strictly prohibited by law.

Cover design by Shay Culligan
Author photo by Harrah Lord
Cover Art © Dudley Zopp, *Phosphors Red,* 2023,
digital alteration of *Phosphors #4,* oil on birch panel, 24 x 20 inches.

ISBN: 978-1-63980-318-7

Library of Congress Control Number: 2023935849

Kelsay Books
502 South 1040 East, A-119
American Fork, Utah 84003
Kelsaybooks.com

*To my husband Roger Leddington,
who unfailingly believes that I can swim for miles,
walk across fiery lava flows, write poetry,
and stay young forever.*

Magma intrusions are formed by fluid volcanic matter that penetrates the spaces between local rocks. These super-heated igneous intrusions crystallize from the molten magma and can been seen in black or white lines that write their story on the granite of Maine's coastlines. I've been obsessed with volcanoes since childhood and traveled all over the world to witness eruptions. Yet in Maine, where I've lived for 50 years, I have to go back 500 million years to connect with a time when volcanoes were active. As I trace the lines of magma intrusions with my bare toes on Maine's rocky shores, I think of what lies below the surface—the hot spots that shape and form the geology not only of the land but also of a life.

Contents

SECTION I

Almost the Last Billboard in Maine	13
Eruption	17
The Goddess Speaks	19
Five hundred million years before	20
Every Map Is Both Illusion and Illustration	22
Ice Out on a River in Maine	23
Roadside Geology	24
State of Being	26
Her Skates	29
Moon Shot	30
Chess Match	32
The Beach at Patchogue	34
A Dropped Stitch	36
Subterranean Homesick Blues Revisited	38
Gun Shy Little Sister	40
Cigarettes and Clay	41

SECTION II

Shiksa	43
No Names on the Trees	47
There is No Bad Light to Make a Photograph	48
The Sign Reads: Prophesies Are Coming True	49
I'm Sick of This	50
Swimming to the Moon	52
Whooper Swans	54
Starlight Striptease	55
Maine Winter	56
Pandemic Shadows	58
Invaders	60

Cicadas Don't Wear Heels	62
Tectonic	63
Highway 137: The Red Road	64
Fagradalsfjall Pilgrimage	65
All Day I Wandered Winter Woods	67
Arctic Terns	68

SECTION III

Lost Songs	69
Sicily	72
Meteorites in Bethel Maine	74
Moon Wobble	76
Petra	77
Elegy for Halemaumau	78
Torch Ginger	79
Damariscotta Salt Marsh	80
Liminal Time	81
My Nephew Asks, If You Knew You Were Dying ___Would You Jump into a Lava Lake?	83

SECTION I

Almost the Last Billboard in Maine

—in 1984

The Highway Beautification Act of '64
banning billboards on interstate highways,
was the passionate wish of Lady Bird Johnson:
& LBJ said to his aides, *I love this woman;
so you will see that we win.*

Maine's law passed in '78:
banning billboards from all roads.
It took six years to enact.

Almost the last billboard stood alone
on Route One
opposite the plant where I worked;
young, a vice president
in a company
that processed thousands of rolls of film
for LaVerdiere's and Wellby's and Rexall.

Recently divorced, I'd begun to date.
I called him "the electrician"
though his name was Bob.

One morning I drove to the plant,
across the highway, next to an ad for Merit
cigarettes, appeared a new billboard:

a hand-painted picture of a volcano,
crude, a lumpy black mountain
& above it a clump of gray cloud;

sides flowed with poster-paint lava.
Beside this, the words:
Imperspicuous, NEVER!
$\qquad\qquad\qquad$ *Love, Bob.*

Everyone knew it was for me;
factory workers giggled. My boss called me
in to his office.   *Who's Bob?* he winked.

The radio station picked it up:
the whole town was talking.
Who knows what *imperspicuous* means?

Me, I knew. Our imperspicuous romance
had begun on Route 1 towards Wells,
where we stopped at a used bookstore.

I bought a tattered book of old words & read
to him while he drove—*imperspicuous:
vague, uncertain, unclear.* He said it described

me to a T; might be how I felt about him.
His painting was the last volcanic eruption
ever seen in Maine;

on almost the last billboard, for me.

Eruption

After school, I sat at the kitchen table.
My mother smoked Camel cigarettes and drank coffee,
I ate the oatmeal cookies she'd baked for me.

What did you learn today? she asked.

We got in trouble in English class, talking,
I have extra homework: an essay
on Transcendentalism, what's that?

The encyclopedia will tell you, look it up.

She knew but didn't want to make it easy.
She pulled Whitman off the shelf and read:

As I wend to the shores I know not . . .

She noticed my attention wander.
And how about science?
A professor of chemistry, she always probed.

Geology, Mom, do you know about volcanoes?

Opening a *National Geographic,* she flipped
the yellow-bordered cover directly to the photograph
I'll never forget: a two-page spread
of Surtsey erupting from under the sea.
The coffee boiled over on the stove.

I grabbed the magazine. Red lava,
flowing down black slopes and dripping
over black cliffs into an angry sea.
An island rising like a rabbit pulled from a magic hat
in the middle of the Atlantic.

Nature here in sight of the sea taking advantage of me . . .

Look at the date, she said.

To dart upon me and sting me,

I turned twelve on the day
that Surtsey was born: November 15, 1963.
I'll never forget the image, the smell—
burnt coffee merged with sulfur.

Because I have dared to open my mouth to sing at all.

The fire god Surtr called, something erupted
within me, and I began to sing.

The Goddess Speaks

At the edge of the crater, call out my name,
honor me as Pelehonuamea,
the fires of the earth, the wind on the oceans,
I wield my power in the color red.

Red like lehua blossoms encircling my neck
flowers left as an offering at the edge of the crater
Red as the color that grows on my cheeks
feel my hand on your back, look up to the sky,
see my blush in the funneling clouds.

Red like the dark veins of a drinking man's nose
Dirty hands, whiskey breath on the back of your neck
Read like a diary whose lock he has broken
Red is the blood that flows between your legs
Red as the shame of unwashed stains

Red bursts of anger flush through my face,
I stamp my feet, I make the earth tremble
In a flaming display, I'll destroy these men's houses
watch their dreams disappear in curses of red,
feel the danger that dazzles in blue methane flames.

Now see my beauty in pyrocumulous clouds, I'll heal
the earth with a rain of green olivine crystals—
destruction, creation, all is the same—
Wounds now healed over, red rocks in the mirror
reborn as hibiscus, anthurium, torch ginger

Honor the earth, call out my name,
honor my body, draped in dark, flowing red.

Five hundred million years before

I was born from the sea, made of stars,
to trace a path across the earth
on footprints of fire.
A sea was here before this sea
now visible in rocks,
mountains, quarries, and sand
of limestone, schist and shale.
Once lava flourished, formed island
arcs, those distant mountains
mostly washed away.
Continents collided, as the Iapetus
Ocean slid into the lithosphere
plunging downward to the East.
Another ocean formed, the one
I learned to swim in,
the sweet and sometimes violent
tumult of the waves; the Atlantic
wedged between America and Europe.
Glaciers retreated stranding erratic rocks,
their sculptural presence to remind
us of absence; icy ancestors carved
out rocks and waterfalls.
I arrived in Maine in '74 amidst
a recession, no jobs to be found.
We lived on food stamps in a winter rental
at the edge of the ocean, the granite
outreach home to seals in winter.

I had nothing but time:
time to pick rose hips from shoreline shrubs,
make jam, knead yeast and flour, bake bread,
and sew. Time to photograph, make prints
in the darkroom, and wonder.
I worried about no job, no money.
A wise friend said to me, *don't worry
about the money, worry about time.
You'll never have it again like this.*
So much of it. So few demands.

Every Map Is Both Illusion and Illustration

My first volcano-love was Surtsey
the island born on my twelfth birthday,
breeching the waves along the Mid-Atlantic Ridge,
rupturing the surface, revealing
underwater stitches: Earth's seams.
I was an adolescent. My family felt crazy.
I saw the photo in the magazine.
Later, I started to dream of a journey
that would beckon me far from home.
First to Iceland, on that mid Atlantic ridge;
then to Alaska, with my second husband,
where I discovered this map in the USGS gift shop
of the Alaskan Volcano Observatory.
It traces lines of plate tectonics.
Black dots mark earthquake zones;
each tiny red dot is a volcano.
Not folded and tucked in the glove compartment,
to show me which route
will get me where I want to go,
it lives on the wall of my office
held up by push pins over my desk
stretched wider than my arms can reach—
tall enough to stare down at me.
In the center—the Pacific Ocean—undivided—
back East, we never saw the Earth this way,
its fontanelle, its skull complete.

Ice Out on a River in Maine

Just married, we bought a summer camp
on a river between two dams. Summer's
water moved slowly, we fished and swam;
added insulation, covered windows
with plastic, wrapped the pipes with heat tape.
With winter's cold winds the river froze. We
filled plastic jugs at the town hall and hauled
water in on a sled to wash our dishes.

The river ice shifted, groaned, and cracked at night.
Screeching like a wild beast. By day, we skated
silent on its surface, keeping close to shore.
While the center current flowed swiftly,
sometimes we had to skate across thin ice
to get home. In spring the ice broke—branches
and trees floated past; a bucket, a couch,
and a bed swept by on the raging waters.

Tim and his friend Butch took the canoe
to run the rapids while I read a book. Spring
filtered through plastic still wrapped on the windows.
Until the hospital called.
Flipped canoe, lucky rescue, hypothermia.
All while I read a book never thinking
the course of my life might change
that spring with the ice going out.

Roadside Geology

a pantoum

I.

after my first marriage

Geologists try to decipher ancient stones. Mysteries remain.
Continents collided, broke apart, drifted, lifted into mountains.
Sea creatures fossilized in mountain peaks—distant chaos of time
Maine is an intricate collage of fragments.

Continents collided, broke apart, drifted, lifted into mountains
50 years ago—starry eyed—we drifted up the road to Maine
Maine is an intricate collage of fragments—we
winterized a cabin on the river, hauled our water in by sled.

50 years ago—starry eyed—we drifted up the coast to Maine
meandering through the muddy sediments of youth—we
winterized a cabin on the river, hauled our water in by sled;
wood stove bellowed smoke; frost obscured the windowpanes.

Meandering through the muddled sentiments of youth
we broke apart, drifted, and lifted on our different paths—
fragmented memories fossilized—the distant chaos of our lives.
Geologists try to decipher ancient stones. Mysteries remain.

Lines 1 and 4 of the first stanza are taken from Roadside Geology of Maine *by D.W. Caldwell*

II.

after my second marriage

Geologists try to decipher ancient stones. Mysteries remain.
The coast of Maine parallels abundant faults that fracture
Earth's crust—more than 200 islands appear in Casco Bay—
their origins in bands of rocks eroded by the wind and waves.

Parallel to abundant faults that fracture Earth's crust
herons stalk fish in tidal pools—our island home in Casco Bay
among the 200 islands that dot the bay—we built
a house to command the view—of osprey and herons

that stalk fish in tidal pools—our island home in Casco Bay
rarely at home, I worked long hours, I sought success—we
built a house to view the changing tides, the wind and waves,
we raised the roof, built up three floors to command the view

Rarely at home, I worked long hours, I sought success—we
raised the roof, built up three floors to command the view
abundant faults fractured the peaceful scene of birds on wing
receding tides revealed weak rocks. Mysteries remain.

State of Being

on the occasion of Maine's bicentennial

as if
        Maine was born into this world
        in a moment of consecration:
                      statehood

as if
people of the Dawnland weren't here thousands of years before
                the French
                      and English
                                arrived from foreign shores
Wabenaki hunted giant beavers in a time when
                          wooly mammoth roamed
     fished salmon in these rivers   harvested the shellfish
        now fried up for tourists at Ken's Clam Shack
              discovered   in middens   evidence
            of forgotten stories

as if
        the rocks weren't alive millions of years before us
and the sea creatures   fossilized   into mountains
        hadn't lived on the floor
                          of the Iapetus Ocean
        an ocean consumed
                into the earth's mantle
                              millions of years ago

as if
        the ocean was always the Atlantic
                    that crashes into our rocky coast
and oceans didn't open and close
     like the convenience store on the corner of Union and Elm.

as if
   the oceans left limestone reefs
           offshore islands
distant in time
   left their magma chambers behind as granite plutons
      for us to build our buildings
         our monuments
              glorifying what?

what if
   the Somali immigrants who fled their homelands
      to settle in Lewiston

   all those who washed up on our shores
      were given blankets and maize,
         and taught how to survive a Nor'Easter

what if
   we were all still a part   not apart
   one world—one supercontinent like Pangea
   with no boundaries for Africa, Europe,
         North or South America

   no walls   we act as if

we had nothing to do with the extinction of song

   if Rachel Carson hadn't warned us of our poisons
   I wouldn't float on the lake carved out by a glacier
   and watch an eagle swoop down to see if I am a fish . . .

               we act as if

deaths of songbirds, plastic reefs on the oceans,
    unbreathable air   fires burning vast tracts of land

    as if we had nothing to do with any of this.

As if our death, our deaths,

        even our extinction
matters to the rocks that move so slowly we don't think

        they are alive

pacing themselves to cover our bones
   creating new lands   in their own time

    in their own statehood.

Her Skates

I picture my mother perched
at the end of a dock—her skates—now mine—
kicking into the air—her arms reaching
to the sky in joyous anticipation
of gliding across the ice,
spinning, smiling, skating
in crisp wintry air.

In my twenties I skated on river ice so black
I could see leaves float downstream beneath my feet.
Thick ice at the edges, open water in the center channel,
we cut our marks on polished mirrors believing
our lives would last forever.

I lace up my skates—her skates—
with torn white leather toes
new laces replace the old knotted ones
too frayed to support my older ankles,
unaccustomed as I am now to standing
on a single sharp edge.

I walk onto the pond, conquering
fears of falling by conjuring her joy,
until I am sailing—arms spread wide,
side-stepping leaves, cracks, bubbles
in the uneven ice, feeling the past slide by
on each single glide of the blade.

Moon Shot

The summer men landed on the moon
I launched from my family in Connecticut,
drove 2,452 miles with my friend Candy
in her car named Mortimer, and landed
at Reed College in Portland, Oregon
under a cloud of drizzling August rain.
Letters from home were already waiting
for me, and more arrived daily with men-
on-the-moon stamps, planting our flag
238,900 miles away from earth. Perhaps
I needed to be that far away to keep myself
from getting pulled back in by the gravity
of my mother's letters: *Air Mail, Fair Mail,
Share Mail, Bare Mail, Scare Mail, Beware
Mail.* Always signed *the White Queen*
after the character in Alice's Wonderland,
who, befuddled, would believe each day
six impossible things before breakfast.
Like my mother: the impossible demons
she fought—with a pot of coffee, two packs
of cigarettes, daily doses of Valium. On torn
steno paper, red pen, red ink, she scrawled
her heart out, wrote of my sister trying
to fit into skirts I left behind, of my brother
visiting dear Dr. Dulit twice a week to treat
depression—and dodge the draft. Of battles
with my father, desperate to find herself.

She told me Daddy didn't think she should
have let me go so far away. But sometimes,
she wrote, you have to cut the cord—again,
and again, and again. She told me to save
her letters—each one got darker, my tears
welled up—black ink, blurred words—I didn't
understand until years later:
nothing a 17-year-old girl could do but
fly to the moon or head back home again.

Chess Match

He played in competitions—blindfolded
against the clock, and won. 30 games simultaneously
and he won. He won in the chess club, the regional
tournament—he strove to be a master of the game.

I heard the clink of ice before he closed his study door,
lit his pipe, and studied the board, while smoke billowed
out into the hall. I hid in my room, watchful for
his heavy footstep on the stair that meant he'd been interrupted
and came out looking for someone to blame.

On rare occasions when he had the patience
to teach me the game, I learned the moves.
The opening gambit—moving my pawn
2 spaces forward and then my knight
2 up, 1 to the side. He took my pieces one by one,
while I retreated from the final threat—a bishop,
a rook, or a queen, moved into place, my pieces
strewn aside, my defenses crumbled, and I could see
the checkmate in his next move.

The chess tournament dinner was a gala event,
he'd earned the trophy, and my mother insisted
that I come. I was sixteen, maybe seventeen,
and wore a dress I'd made—that made my father
raise his heavy eyebrows, frown, and look away—
a white satin miniskirt, spaghetti straps, Eugene McCarthy
for President buttons printed on the fabric.
Long hair trailing down my back, I danced the twist—
all night, I danced with every older man who asked.

At home that night and every night, he shut the door,
let smoke seep out—while I went off and marched
against the war. We didn't meet across
the checkered squares to play by any rules he knew.

He loved his chess, controlling pieces across the board.
I learned the moves, but never any strategy except defense.
I didn't understand the Queen was the most valuable piece, free
to move wherever she wanted, fast or slow, while the king
was constrained to one square at a time.

The Beach at Patchogue

The family campfire sheds its sepia light
on woven picnic baskets strewn at random
and narrow pickets with spindly spikes
to keep the dunes from washing out to sea.

The gathered women, now grainy, not quite in focus,
yet clearly my mother and her clan
have coffee boiling on the fire. An unused skillet
from lunch or dinner lies forgotten in an empty basket.
All is silenced by the ocean's waves.

Wearing a cap-sleeved printed dress,
hair pulled back by a headband,
only my mother turns to face the camera.
Smiling, she looks directly at me
as if I'm the photographer here,
the one behind the lens,
and she knows it even then,
long before I come into the picture.

Across the fire, my grandmother sits,
knocking back something stronger than coffee.
Her skirt's hiked up mid-thigh,
one arm's draped around a sister
who stares demurely at the ground.
They remain oblivious to the shutter's click.

They don't see they will all outlive my mother.

It will be after she marries, returns to the shore,
teaches her children to swim in the waves.
After she brings us here in the night to build a fire
and fills our heads with Scandinavian stories
of trolls under bridges.

After she's gone, I will find this long-forgotten photo,
see the campfire sparks trail across the sky,
and taste the salt of the sea.

A Dropped Stitch

My hem stitches were sloppy—
impatiently sewn to finish an A-line skirt
for Home Economics, and get back to playing
kickball with the boys on the street.

I didn't know that other girl, who at my age
sailed far from familiar paths of a Lithuanian village
whose name I still don't know, to land in New York
where buildings were taller than trees and rivers
of people rushed by speaking languages she did not understand,
understanding only that here there were no pogroms.

She knew how to sew and how to see,
picked up work in the garment district.
she could make a dress after a single sight.
They sent her to the fashion shows, no pencil
allowed, she would come back and duplicate
the high fashion dresses at a fraction of the cost.

When I was older she made my only prom dress,
for a winter cotillion, so I could dance
in long-sleeved red velvet while the snow
fell outside, and my brown hair swung long
and free, and some unremembered boy's hands
rested upon my soft waist of luxury.

I never wondered about the girl who learned
to make the delicate stitches that caressed my skin.
I knew her as that grandmother of unfamiliar dishes
like chopped liver and potato latkes, of kugel and cookies
without chocolate. She cooked and sewed and I never asked her
when or how or why she traveled so far from home.

When I visited her once in the home for the aged,
after she'd buried both sons, my father and his brother,
she was angry at God, for not taking her instead,
angry she hadn't escaped the pogroms of fate.
She told me not to stay long that the aides stole
your underwear if you didn't move quickly. Go now,
she said, you are far too young for this place.

Subterranean Homesick Blues Revisited

Wafts of English Leather drift under my door.
My brother Bob is in the living room, Dylan's on
the stereo, loud. "Johnny's in the basement,
mixing up the medicine." I hear the bass voice
of his friend Joe Louis, tall, black, and handsome.
I'm wide-eyed and tongue-tied
when he stops to say hello.

    Look out, kid.

Bob's dressed in striped bell-bottom jeans,
long curling hair reaching his shoulders,
the smell of liquor on his breath. They say
they'll take Mommy's new car—
the one she begged Daddy to let her buy—
the MG Midget in British racing green
that smells like fresh leather, the real
English kind. I'll keep a lookout,
hoping no one comes home and I'm asked
where they've gone.

    Look out, kid.

I hear the tune of "Subterranean Homesick Blues"
when my mother writes in her letters:
Daddy's on the wagon
eating just tomatoes.
Bob was on the toilet
shooting bags of heroin.
Nancy's locked her bedroom door,
eating hordes of candy corn.
Aunt Ossie came to visit—
we're playing tennis and drinking gin.

I hum to myself:
It's something you did
God knows when,
but you're doing it again.
You better run across the country
looking for a new friend.

   Look out, kid.

Gun Shy Little Sister

We're both in black cowboy hats
only he's staring down the barrel
of his gun—one eye closed—ready
to fire at whoever crosses his path.
He's always been the gunslinger
in our not-so-OK corral, quick to anger,
taking the hard road, blazing a trail.

I am shyly fingering this weapon
still in its holster. I am thankful he kept
our enemies engaged, while I figured out
a different track. In another shot, I'm wearing
a single feather in a band around my head.
I tried on many hats before I found my poet's cap.
Always staying out of the line of fire.

Cigarettes and Clay

Too small to contain it all
my clothes cycle through the seasons
from bedroom to spare room and back
discarding those I no longer need or want.

At the back of the spare room closet
grief hangs in the old wool shirt
handsewn with pewter reindeer
buttons. It never moves.

I remember your closet stayed
untouched for a year. The blue
velour pants-set draped shapelessly
over a hanger.

The little black dress I wanted
to wear when I was fifteen
and you said I was too young.

Dad's next wife cleaned
out the closet. Your plaid shirt the
only remnant I saved from Goodwill.

I bought black dresses for every occasion
each one given away while the shirt has stayed
hanging for 50 years now.

Your scent woven into the fabric
Camel cigarettes, potter's clay, and Chanel—
those buttons my prayer beads.

SECTION II

Shiksa

The term for my mother;
her best friend Jane told me stories.
She'd met my mother pushing baby
carriages in garden apartments
in northern New Jersey, licking ice cream
cones and talking.

My father's family sat *shiva:*
treated him as dead. Married by
a judge, she didn't meet his parents.
A rift too wide to find a bridge to cross.
Jane's husband was Jewish too, but
his family welcomed her with open arms.

As a child I made a nativity diorama:
Bethlehem, a blue construction paper sky
and a six-pointed star.
My father got angry; he said it didn't belong.
I thought: neither do I.

Later: After my parents died much too young,
Jane told me the story of Aunt Ossie:
for her college graduation she wanted
her brother and his *shiksa* wife invited.
My mother borrowed a dress from Jane,
and went to meet her in-laws.

But Aunt Ossie told me it differently:
She said my grandmother snuck out
to see her grandchildren on the Sabbath
while her husband was at temple.
Finally. She said, "Enough. I want these
children welcomed." She wanted us.

The boundaries of our family realigned.
I remember those few visits, before
my grandfather died:
he'd reach into his pockets
and give us silver dollars.

Ossie was the last to go.
At the Hebrew cemetery, the rabbi spoke
Thou preparest a table before me in the presence of mine
   enemies . . .
We unveiled her headstone
Surely goodness and mercy shall follow me all the days of my life—

Wandering through the markers,
so many graves bore our surname
stone faces of family I'd never known.

No Names on the Trees

I'm hoarding gold these days
the backlit leaves of maple and oak
clinging to branches before the wind
pries them loose and strips
the color from the sky.

I'm grasping the last light of each day
before we change the clocks and it's dark
in the afternoon, and dark when I awake.
I'm trying to hitch a ride on the tail
of our sun 93 million miles away.

I just found out that my father's cousin
had five children who perished
in the Holocaust. No names on the family tree,
just five small asterisks. My father never told us.
This news crashes into me, leaving me searching
for buried names in the fallen leaves.

I think of the teenager Greta who is taking us to task
for robbing her of her future, valuing the pursuit of gold
more than the preservation of the wild, plundering
the Amazon rainforest, ploughing under our primeval
forests, leaving a desiccated inheritance

the missing trees that should belong to her
this wobbling planet that gives
me such moments as these
seeing gold in the maple leaves.

clinging to the fading light
knowing darkness will fall
hoping it will be illuminated
    by at least one star
        but I'm wishing for five stars.

There is No Bad Light to Make a Photograph

—Advice from the Natural Eye workshop with Eddie Soloway

Notice the shadows play on the pavement
in the harsh light of midday the leaves
become coins thrown in the street,
imagination stretches as afternoons elongate
tree trunks take their turn in the spotlight.

Evening comes and the sun disappears
in a soft haze of color—even the sunset
blurs into scattered light
civil twilight, nautical twilight,
astronomical twilight,
finally darkness falls.

In Alaska once, I left Wasilla to drive past Fairbanks
destination a place with wooden hot tubs, winter nights,
aurora emblazoned across the sky, but midday, midway,
darkness fell like a band of robbers stealing daylight
just past Denali, where the road was empty
and snow was falling fast.

I gripped the wheel and kept on going until
the first motel I found, never reaching that perfect
pool, that perfect night, those northern lights
understanding darkness for the first time
lonely, fear of slipping into the night
and no one knowing I went missing.

The Sign Reads: Prophesies Are Coming True

The moon and Mars peered through sixty-foot
pines in night's dark poetry.

Something wild awakened me—screeching coyotes pouncing
on prey? The moon appeared as olivine crystals glowing gold

from a meteor's crash. The largest meteor to hit the earth
in Namibia heated sand so hot it fused into blown glass—

yellow orbs in the desert—visits from the stars—
my startled eyes open—the dream doctor's voice lingers—

—*she is on the final elevator ride down*—

my friend stands as tall as the King's Pines, irreverent
as a circus of squirrels launching from delicate limbs,

full of truth only a true friend speak. She's been by my side
for decades of tangled travels, now at the end of her journey—

will she stay with me as the glimmering magneto-
rotational swirl around the black hole in my galaxy?

I'm Sick of This

Getting up in the middle of the night
I need my uninterrupted night's sleep
so I can do my job where everyone
wants to put their problems in my hands
as if I can fix anything

I don't need that from you too

I don't know why I'm expected to be
empathetic or nurturing or even a good cook
just because I was born with an X instead of a Y
I never wanted to be a teacher or a nurse
and I wondered what in hell I would do with a college degree
I never wanted to be a therapist a psychologist
or even a doctor with all that tending to sickness
although I could get into the diagnosing giving
my opinion and especially the illegible handwriting

I don't need that from you

so don't keep waking me up
in the night with your plaintive cry
making me grudgingly leave the comfort
of my dreams my blanket my pillow so that you
won't decide that inside is just as good as outside
after all that training I have to take you out
and all you do is munch on the grass and sniff
each of the dandelions gone to seed in the
garden and I watch you wander over to the
wisteria arbor that has fallen to the
ground and needs to be propped up

you sit down and I follow your gaze to
the heavens filled with stars
and I take a moment to
inhale the scent of night
before I gather you
in my arms and
take you back
to bed.

Swimming to the Moon

—After a painting by David Graeme Baker

Is the lake ever really that color?
The green of mallards and shimmering.
Edges of loon-black, white rings radiating.

Four boys swimming, naked torsos,
capes of moonshine. Wet skin
and innocence.

I love to swim, naked, water on skin
mornings before dawn, slipping in,
water, reflecting sky, soft blue or pink with first light.

Often the moon is still over the hills,
but the lake has never been that shade of green.
Perhaps it happens only at night

when I'm asleep and dreaming,
the moonlight's magic shining,
peacocks strut from the hills,

shed their feathers, and the water
becomes a cloak of green.
Last night the loons woke me at midnight

trilling their calls—insistent, penetrating
sleep—the moon halfway to full.
I skipped over granite boulders

to find the water's edge,
don the cloak of peacock feathers
to waltz with the moon and stars.

A rhythm as deep as the sky was dark,
drumbeat rolling in with daybreak's clouds
rain drops waking me with morning.

Whooper Swans

The day filled with wild swans
in the skies and in the ponds—

a memory of driving, fall, mountains
and fjords of Iceland, ice forming

on mountain passes, a family
of Whooper swans climbed up

on too-thin ice one by one,
struggling yet graceful, moving across.

Another memory—walking, spring,
southern Iceland. The pond no more

than a puddle. Strong wings bristled
at my intrusion, rushed from the brush

to enter the water, swam in circles, each
movement an arc of grace, thrusting

his neck forward, gliding his full white body
back and forth, his eyes on me

a movement—a female Phalarope leaves her nest
in the grass beside the pond. Could the swan

be protecting her not-yet-hatched young?
I envy this—protection to save my nests

of ideas unhatched that may never be born
without the strength of powerful wings.

Starlight Striptease

—for Connie

At the entrance to the Starlight motel,
the roadside sign flashed Chippendales Tonight!
Moths circled the yellow lamplight while I stood waiting
for someone I'd only just met, a party for a bachelorette

inside, women sat chugging down beers and stuffing singles
in g-strings of men thrusting their hips to Sinatra's song
New York, New York, in this rural Maine town, smelling of
cigarettes, peanuts, stale beer and the start of a friendship.

Men danced in and out of our lives, three husbands for me,
she married just one, though once she had a lover who drank
too much and waved a gun in the air. So many two-steps,
too many missteps.

Stung by the jellyfish in Baja, whitewater rafting a river
in Colorado, running from the ash of Arenal volcano, we
waltzed down the aisles of a supermarket in Taos,
and camped under a canvas of stars far from home
the night my nephew was born.

I read the Tarot cards for her, predicting
nothing,
but telling all.

Maine Winter

November

Slanted light gilds tree trunks
in disappearing daylight
the creeping lengths of shadows
echoing in the bay. I've always
been drawn to the sea—the smoke
that rises off the water when the air
grows cold, the water still warm.
The sea brought you to me.

December

Cold rain, the temperature drops
and suddenly trees are glazed
in ice. Sun shimmering through a forest
and the world stays frozen
as glittering time stops in prisms
of glass leaves. At night the full moon
spotlights the branches. You and I walk
out in slippers to gaze at the sky.

January

You sit on the shore and I skate onto
the frozen ice—a mirror with deep traces
of white lines—a Miro canvas with patches of blue
sky on the black and white pond
quenching my thirst for the perfect ice
beneath the blades of my skates,
you watch from shore as I glide past.

February

Midwinter night and we're driving home.
Time warps when you put the high beams on,
watch the snow swirl blinding white flakes
in every direction across a black tunnel
of time unending as the road disappears
we're lost in a blizzard of memories—
those we've shared about driving in the snow,
lost or afraid or alone or with another,
and those we haven't shared: of past loves
falling in and out of love's grasp, and why,
why now, I am feeling awe looking out
of the grimy windshield of an SUV hurtling
along a country road, trees lurching into view,
fence posts dragging past. We are lost in this
moment. Only this moment. With you alone.

Pandemic Shadows

Dense pines drape the path in shadow
shafts of slanted sunlight filter through branches
falling upon a six-foot span of planks across
a once-muddy section of trail, now dusted in snow,
I see a coffin in a cathedral of shades.

I had a call this morning from Ada.
Her cousin, dead from an overdose. Drugs
laced with Fentanyl. She said the funeral was yesterday.
You know, the walk-through kind they do nowadays.
I don't know. I haven't been to a funeral in the pandemic.

I picture Ada dressed in black, wearing
her black mask, marching past the casket,
six feet behind the next person in line,
driving home and sitting alone in her
darkened living room with the shades drawn.

My friend Kath died in December,
her children have decided to wait until summer
for any kind of service, but I think that by summer this
wound will be imperfectly healed over with scars.
This incomplete mourning will take its toll.

In the woods, I reach for my iphone to take a picture,
Kath's name pops up under My Favorites. I want to call. I want
to hear her tell me she's OK, and ask how I'm doing. Always she
turned the focus on me, even while she was facing the limits
of time, the clock ticking faster and faster towards the day when
she could no longer hold me, or anyone she loved.

I read on my screen that a star dying soon after the beginning
of the universe could be disrupting mobile phone reception today.
Kath could be calling me across the span of time and space,
but I can't hear her, the phone reception disrupted by this
giant explosion of matter.

Invaders

Battling an invasion
that came from the Himalayas
crossed the mountains of Kashmir
journeyed here to Maine.

Disguised by many names
I've been calling it Jewel-weed
but it turns out that it's
Impatiens Glandulifera (a purple flower)

Jewelweed is Impatiens Capensis
with its orange flowers,
or Impatiens Pallida
(yellow flowers) all
beginning with impatience—
Mine.

Undercover as Himalayan Balsam
Touch-me-nots
Kiss-me-on-the-mountain
Gnome's hatstand
Copper tops, Indian balsam
Policeman's Helmet, Bobby Tops,
Jumping Jack . . .

Did I say Gnome's hatstand?
I like that one.

These hooded flowers
colonize disturbed habitats
another name for our garden
once home to tall oaks and maples

that keep reseeding
trying to root out dirt beneath
our tomatoes, eggplants,
roses and herbs.

pollinated by bees
and hummingbirds
Impatiens can fertilize themselves
without ever exchanging pollen—
aggressive competitors
excreting toxins to weed out
competitors we're trying to grow.

Recommended remedy: pulling
and cutting, manual tasks,
Sisyphean fight to hold the line
against the invasion—
not my strength I dare say
I tire of the effort
to keep it away

Look at its strong points:
you can make parfait or jam
use it to relieve itching and pain
feed the bees and the hummingbirds
and strangle the notion
of any control
over "our" backyard.

Cicadas Don't Wear Heels

for Laura

They don't need to wear stilettos
males court the females with a chorus
of throaty hums—billions of Brood X
emerge near Laura in Princeton.

Each day she records the magic of music
growing louder. Magicada Periodical Cicada
(some say See-kah-duh, some say See-kay-duh
Like some say to-may-to and some say to-mah-to).

A sexy, salsa dance, an orgy of reproduction,
red eyes glowing, lurid wings rustling,
hips thrusting, males drumming,
their breeding cycle a phenom of sex

recorded in the annals of university lore.
Buried underground for seventeen years.
What were you doing seventeen years ago?
Wearing heels and make-up? Dancing up a storm?

What's been feeding underground that might
be aching to burst forth at any moment
in an abundance of ecstasy?

We spent almost 17 months buried
in our houses, fearful of the virus,
while pandemic raged across the globe,
and now we're stepping out.

Advertising tells us we're roaring back,
1920s style, an orgy of extravagance,
But some of us still shyly greet strangers,
still wear our masks, and look outside in gleeful
pleasure at bugs dancing our eruption of desire.

Tectonic

> 1. *relating to the structure of the earth's crust and the large scale processes which take place within it.*
> 2. *a change or development very significant or considerable.*

1.

I've been obsessed since I was thirteen with a single image of the eruption of Surtsey off the coast of Iceland. A tongue of lava pushes back the waves, an island appears from nowhere. It rises along a fault line that intersects the Earth like a seam sewn by a seamstress with a shaky hand, jutting this way and that, bisecting the globe into plates that collide against one another or rip open the ocean floor to spill blood and tear the Earth apart beneath the sea. The plates move at the speed your fingernails grow, slowly, inexorably tearing Iceland in two, one side moving towards Europe, the other drifting over to North America.

2.

I'm sheltered-in for months as a pandemic spreads across the globe, the world, it seems, erupts in protest over centuries of subjugation, the flora and fauna spiral towards extinction. I look out from windows that I've spent the past month washing. My world appears bubble-wrapped in endless Amazon packaging stretched around the fenced-in yard. Each morning rose-colored light dances with the shadows on my closet doors. Giant heads of peonies nod into bloom, a robin steals the worms from our first vegetable garden, newly planted. The evening news shouts from the large-screen TV—this is what's happening—forces me to look, until I shut it off and go to bed. At night the virus slips past my dreamcatcher and enters my dreams. "You are going to die," the doctor tells me, then asks "How do you feel about that?" I answer, "I am OK with death. Just not today."

My cocoon of beauty holds still while the earth shifts.
Imperceptible. Momentous.

Highway 137: The Red Road

Lean with me into the curves
he instructed before we began
my first motorcycle ride: the glee
of children from the sixties, now almost 60.

On the Red Road from Kalapana to Kopoho,
my arms wound tight around his waist,
we swerved around each bend
my hair whipping against my face.

Glimpses of ocean ravaging black lava
cliffs—mile marker 13 flashed by
blue sky, blue water,
red road reflected
my blue eyes gleaming.

At night, he whispered,
"I am not your true love,"
but I didn't believe him.
Enticing scents of sulfur flew in the bedroom
window inhabiting the arms of my dreams.

I flew back home to Maine before
the white Lexus veered into a turn
and cut in front of his Harley,
catapulting the bike and body
into that blue sky forever
changing the geography of my life.

Years later, I watched the evening news
as a wall of lava two stories high
snaked across Highway 137 halting
traffic, consuming cars, houses,
and mile marker 13.

Fagradalsfjall Pilgrimage

Pilgrimage: n. a long journey, undertaken as a quest or for a votive purpose

My life has been a pilgrimage of sorts
this obsession with volcanoes since childhood
to see the earth in liquid fire, to witness primal
movement, beginning and ending of time.

I climb the mountain, head bowed
paying attention to the narrow path beneath
my feet, my boot treads worn from many
other climbs. I fall on my knees, they're scraped
and bruised before the steep ascent begins.

An old man passes me, a cane in hand,
white hair blown back he's done this countless
times before—not here perhaps
but other mountains, other quests to see
the earth anew, a different view.

A woman with a baby in a pack in front;
my camera's in my backpack, my tripod slung
across my shoulder, we each have burdens
carried on this journey, this vow
to feel the heat and see the world aflame.

A line of people, multi-hued, move slowly up
the slope is steep, climbing higher, the sun
goes lower, the clouds now shaded orange
in the purple twilight, earth's pulse
visible in the plume that rises to the sky.

Reaching the ridge, the people settle
some spreading blankets, some moving closer

all watching the lava build up in jagged edges
of black cinder cone, until it spills into a river and
thrusts in the air with unspeakable force.

The trek down descends into darkness
Sleet and rain wash us clean for the final half mile.

All Day I Wandered Winter Woods

Camera hung around my neck,
divorced, discouraged, far from home,
questioning the falling dusk
—God or no God?

At midnight, I stumbled
from my cabin into the arctic night
to find a place to pee, looking up
the Talkeetna mountain range loomed black
silhouetted by a glowing green.

Vibrating like the neon lights
of Tokyo's pachinko parlors—
green and pink and purple flashes
pinging steely points of stars
the sky a game of bouncing lights.

Impossible glow, shimmers and smokes
slaps me in the face: this!
the winning number—
stars tumble from above
divinity writ across the sky.

Arctic Terns

In Iceland this spring, arctic terns circle
overhead all day—a day that lasts and lasts
turning twilight towards midnight
fusing pink in pre-dawn light at three.

Fifty thousand miles from Arctic to Antarctica,
Iceland's coast to the Weddell Sea and return.
In a lifetime they might have winged
to the moon and back three times.

Aerodynamic wings slice the wind and clouds,
they soar screeching songs higher and higher—
a breeding dance in this land of moss and tundra,
pumice rocks, and windblown shores.

I hear their voices in my mind as I migrate
home to Maine, imagine the map of their journey,
following across the Atlantic, tracing the coasts
of Africa and South America as if they knew
this route before the continents split.

SECTION III

Lost Songs

In a restaurant in Italy they dine
on songbirds. A delicacy—so delicious
they say—crunching the tiny
bones and heads in their mouths,
spitting out the beaks.

Birds fly paths of migration
traveled for thousands of years,
their routes leading them to us,
trapped in nets and served up
on our tables.

Each year the flocks grow more scant
fainter songs, more haunting.
The delicacy increasingly rare, illicit,
more costly and sought after.
Our greed more evident.

I listen for their ghostly echoes, lost songs
that wander through waves of air,
wondering that I didn't know 'til now—
a third of the birds in the world now gone—
industrial sites once breeding grounds.

While I continue to drive my car,
on routes mere decades old
though I travel far too often.
I'm afraid it may too late, my ears too deaf
to hear our pending extinction.

Sicily

It was a long winter, darkness settled in,
the death toll mounted day by day,
PBS News Hour flashed pictures, a name,
an age, two or three sentences meant to capture
an entire life, and another, and another.

December I descended into darkness.
The one that mattered most to me
dug a hole of silence deep in the ground.
I picked up my phone, saw your name in
My Favorites, began to dial, and put it down.
Now spring arrives with fearsome green leaves.

The lemon trees are blossoming in Sicily.
The restaurant down the street opens in June:
Silician Style special. I pick up my phone again.
Remember when we stayed in the lemon groves
of that village in Sicily? We took the chairlift up
Mt. Etna and walked across black lava fields,

listened to the volcano breathe. Deep breaths.
Remember the sound of breathing?
We watched the movie *Stromboli* with Ingrid Bergman
and Roberto Rossellini. Inspired to see this dark
landscape, we planned a trip to Sicily together.
It was the week before I decided to end my marriage.

You had no idea, yet you understood, in the way
that you had of helping me to see. Never attempting
to change my direction (you said you knew better than that).
Oh how I miss your wisdom.
I miss the scent of lemon trees.

You once told me that when you lose someone you love,
you must open yourself up to love some more. You'd lost
a friend to breast cancer, you brought home her puppy,
and then you reached out to me to take a walk,
and our friendship began.

I have a new puppy this year. I named her after you.
My husband calls her a "pushy broad," but I know
that she simply pushes to get what she wants
what she deserves, what's rightfully hers,
as you always did, and wanted for me.
Etna erupted the week after we left, do you remember?

The trail to the summit closed,
the road we drove up was cut off;
villages on the upper slopes evacuated.
I thought you said it was safe! You said to me,
laughing, shaking your head.
You never really know, I said.

Meteorites in Bethel Maine

Oldest matter we can touch
                                            pieces of dying
stars
                everything is made of this:
            simply star dust.
I pause in the rock museum in Bethel Maine
                    transfixed by crystals in their cases
                        translucent orange
                              gemstones of outer space.
            I'm seeing rocks older than our planet.

Older than the granite of Maine's rocky coast
where my bare toes in summer trace the white lines
of ancient magma intrusions in boulders on the shore.
              I came here to find my footing
              discover my roots in granite plutons
              or tourmaline, Maine's native gem.

                    Instead
                          I'm connected to the stars.
Oh, there's Muonionlustra here!
              10 million years old
                    found in Sweden's Lapland
                        (where my mother's family's from)
A fractured moonrock found in Connecticut
                (where I grew up)

As a child I studied astronomy in summer
            at the Stamford Museum and Nature Center
I begged my parents to buy me a star globe,
                  projecting stars on my bedroom ceiling,
              I slept peacefully tucked in
          under my artificial night sky.

New stars being born in Orion's nebula—
    this comforts me now
            like that blanket of stars in my bedroom.
    I'm feeling small as a gem
    in a fractured universe of time
      that began long before
   and will continue long after
     I've been long gone.

Moon Wobble

In the granite along Maine's coast
white lines of ancient magma
intrude in spaces between
sedimentary rocks.

Liquid fire crystallized,
writ in lines revealing origins
of time, the history
of our planet home.

No lines foretell
our future though—
moon wobble is predicted
in the next decade, our orbits

out of sync—the pull of gravity
lifting tides, thrusting seas
upon the granite shores—ever closer
to disaster as the glaciers melt.

So much has been prophesied
not by some mysterious gods
but by scientists we didn't
have enough faith to believe.

What's that you say? The moon's
been wobbling for centuries,
there's plenty of time to move
to higher ground, to escape

fires and floods, the rising seas.
These lines form a silent sentence
magma's foreshadowing
shrouded in fog.

Petra

I stumbled across it the way you might trip
across trail rock. I was driving
through the East fjords, wending my way
from one village to the next and someone told me
stop in Stodvarfjordur, to see the Petra Stone Museum.

Inside a small house, there's a photo of her, Petra,
stone-sturdy, hauling a bag of rocks like Santa's sack
across her shoulders, hiking through the nearby hills.
She filled the house from floor to ceiling,

gemstones and fossils, minerals
and meteorites, pebbles and boulders tumbled
out into the garden, lined the paths and formed
the patios, filled the shed and paved the drive.
I might have thought she was a hoarder,
the narrowness of passages between
displays and tables filled with specimens,
barely room to eat a meal or chair to sit & read.

This part of Iceland has few roads, the hills remote
and unexplored, her collection contained clues
to the origins of place, the geologic depth of time,
the structure of this earth.

I read a plaque that said the President of Iceland
honored her, and letters from visitors
that say they'd been healed.

Elegy for Halemaumau

For forty years I brought armloads of anthuriums
to the rim of a crater lake far from home, to curry favor
with a youthful goddess. Those sexy, heart-shaped flowers
with penis-like spadix, lay limp against the gaping black
of Halemaumau, hidden beneath a crust, hints of heat
in steam vents and cracks like etchings on the surface.

One night the lava lake broke open and I snuck in
to get the picture. Clouds rising in the night
stars glittering over Mauna Loa like fireflies, my lens
wide open reflecting the red lake and tinted smoke rose
in streaks that appeared like light leaks on an old roll of film.

In the mist of early morning, I watched the sun's first rays
illuminate steam flowing up steep rim walls to shroud
Lehua trees and giant ferns in a golden gauze, stars
faded from the sky while a pale moon set caressing
my bare arms, the sweet scent of hibiscus and bitter
smell of sulfur wrapped around me like a sheet.

Memories now fading to black where that lake once was.
I mourn the earth as it was when I was younger, the lake
now buried, cracked, and broken, words whispered
through a veil of time. My early morning swim in cold
Maine waters wrapped in fog, I hear a trill of loons
and know the past is no longer present.
Today is no better, no worse.

Torch Ginger

My fingers long to touch those desiccated
blooms placed on the crater rim years ago.

The lake was barren then, and parking close,
we walked to the edge to lay our offerings
to Pele. Cliff's edge strewn with bottles of gin—
her favorite, rumor has it—tobacco,
blood-red anthuriums, and torch ginger
for their fiery blossoms on long green stems
rising in gardens to light the sky.

What each supplicant wished for,
I do not know—perhaps a lost love,
or safety from an oncoming storm—
what I wished for—
to know the power of her fires,
to speak the tongues of goddesses
to be the object of desire.

Today the lake is a cauldron
filled with fire that casts
its glow into the night sky
colors the stars as red as torchlight.
But I am far from Pele's ancient home.

I think of loves both found and lost,
words shouted, whispered, or wasted breaths,
fires that raged, ravaged, and roamed,
and remember, that once, I knew desire.

Damariscotta Salt Marsh

Withered grasses fold towards the earth
bleached of color by winter's winds. A horseshoe
crab, its burnished copper shell, buttons protrude
along its spine, its spiky tail no threat—
primeval remains of life abandoned.
The turning of the tide
a ticking metronome of time.
Bubbles rise between the floating floes of ice,
life lies below the surface.

I keep returning in winter
to ruminate among the grasses.
Submerged worlds and whispered words
reflect my losses. Winter's sharp sword edge
of death and grief and loneliness, conceals
the promise that life continues on. Yet color will return
with changing seasons, a flock of wild geese will lead
the incoming tide. I long for spring. It's there—
beneath the surface, emerging.

Liminal Time

The Japanese have a word for it: ma
the space between

empty
but holding

limitless time
all the stars in the universe

   ***

the pause

between inhale
and exhale

rocks covered in seaweed
ebbing the water

between the high tide
and low water line

   ***

spring is meant to arrive
the tree limbs still bare

slate skies promise
more cold rain

I'm forcing forsythia again
bringing spring inside

grasping for morning's dreams
that slip through my fingers

the winter night mind

   ***

when they told my friend
she was going to die, she tuned
out the world

opened her eyes once,
looked at me and said

oh, you're here
and closed them

as if I had interrupted a conversation
at the dinner table
gathering of friends

   ***

I simply sat and held her hand
holding the space

she got on with the business
of dying

My Nephew Asks, If You Knew You Were Dying Would You Jump into a Lava Lake?

A tongue of lava licking the shore,
gulping the ocean in great breaths
photographed in a magazine:
my mother once showed me Surtsey,
an island named for the Norse god of fire,
and emerging from under the sea
on my twelfth birthday.
I tell this story so often
that the tale is knitted together
with threads of fiction and memory
now so intertwined I can no longer
pull them apart. Smoke and incantations,
a spell of land rising from under the sea,
until the island claimed its right to be
on the surface of the earth.

———

My mother built a fire on the beach
and told us stories by its light,
while the smoke wandered through the sky
and sparks flew like fireflies in the night.
She wore the sweater she'd knitted
three times over for my father
who still never wore it.
She said she was like Penelope.
This was years before I knew Penelope
was the long-suffering wife of Ulysses,
and I thought she was just another
bad knitter like my mother.

A chemist and an artist,
she threw pots on a kick wheel in the basement
and painted them with glazes mixed
and fired in the kilns of her imagination.

———

      Would you climb into a coffin
      and slide into the kiln of a crematorium?
      I respond to my nephew.

———

My mother was young when she died,
her heart ripped apart by love's disappointments,
and struggling to claim her own right to be.
Yet the seed was planted for my future odyssey
to travel the world, to witness an eruption,
to capture its essence in a photograph.
That year we went to Iceland,
after her death, after Eldfell's explosion,
there was nothing to see,
but the village of Heimey buried in ash,
and the island of Surtsey beyond reach out to sea.

———

      No really, my nephew persists, but why NOT
      jump into the crater?
      Isn't that the ultimate climax
      for someone who loves volcanoes?

———

I flew to Hawaii when Kilauea burst forth
in a curtain of fire like campfires of war
stretched along miles of earth torn apart,
reft and bereft by forces that couldn't be mended.

Shrouded in smoke, liquid fire
consuming the landscape and folding it over,
black on black forms, braided in ropes
stretching down to the sea
exploding in steam, sparks thrown through the air:
the act of creation extending the land.

> Don't you risk death every time
> you run off to photograph an eruption?
> my nephew wants to convince me of this.

Last year I went to Iceland when
the earth opened up on the edge of a glacier,
melding fire and ice.
I flew next out to Heimay,
climbed the old cinder cone,
and perched atop Eldfell, looked beyond out to sea.
Over the years, waves have softened the edges,
birds nest on its shores, green graces horizons.
Surtsey has changed now,
but the rat-shaped island's still squatting,
fifty years later, still fighting the waves,
and claiming its place.

> That's different, I tell him, wondering how to explain
> life lived close to the edge is not choosing to die.

About the Author

Meg Weston's poetry, non-fiction, and photography express her passion for the geological processes that shape the earth and the stories that shape our lives. Many of her stunning volcanic images can be found on her website www.volcanoes.com.

She is currently the Co-Founder and Director of The Poets Corner, a community-based poetry and prose platform with over 3,000 members, www.thepoetscorner.org. Over the past ten years, she has studied the craft of poetry with such well-known poets as Richard Blanco, Kevin Pilkington, and Ellen Bass among others.

In 2020, Weston released a limited-edition book of poems entitled *Letters from the White Queen,* which includes Weston's poems alongside excerpts of letters written by her mother in 1969 just shortly before her sudden death at the young age of 48. Weston's poems have been published in *Hawaii Pacific Review, Trouvaille Review, The Mountain Troubadour, One Art, Red Fez,* as well as several anthologies.

In January 2020 Weston retired from Maine Media College after eight years as president, where she established The Writers Harbor® program to complement the media arts curricula in photography, filmmaking, and book arts. Weston has been a leader in higher education and led businesses in media and consumer photography including president of *The Portland Press Herald,* president of Konica Corporation's U.S. consumer photofinishing companies, and CEO of PrintLife, an Israeli digital imaging start-up. For 10 years she served as a trustee of the University of Maine System Board of Trustees and served as Chair from 2006–2008.

www.ingramcontent.com/pod-product-compliance
Lightning Source LLC
Chambersburg PA
CBHW030911170426
43193CB00009BA/808